My First Day of Preschool

Written by Amy McDonough

This book belongs to:

____

My First Day of Preschool
Copyright © 2026 by Amy McDonough
All rights reserved.
No part of this book may be reproduced, stored in a retrieval system, or transmitted in any form or by any means — electronic, mechanical, photocopying, recording, or otherwise — without prior written permission from the publisher, except for brief quotations used in reviews.
Published by Rising Butterfly Press
United States
First Edition
ISBN: 979-8-9951646-2-3
Printed in the United States of America

Today is my first day of preschool.
I am so excited!

Mom, my belly hurts.

Do I need to start school today?

I think you are just nervous.
If you are sick,
your teacher will call me.

Are you sure the teacher has a
phone to call you?

Yes dear, if something happens,
they will call me. I will pick you up.

I am Miss Roy.
This is our preschool class!
I am so glad you came!

Everyone has their own cubby.
It will hold all of our things during
the day. Backpacks, coats,
anything we bring.

We will always have bathroom trips. You can ask any time you need to.

First thing we do is circle time.
Calendar, weather, and learning.

We have our own supply boxes at the table for morning lessons. We will learn to cut, write, read, and more!

I have never used scissors before.
Have you guys? I'm nervous.

Great work guys! I am proud of you.
Story time and then outside.

Yay!!!
This is what I have been waiting for!

Be sure to be safe!
Be kind to your friends.
Up ladders and down slides.

This is so much fun!
Structures and room to run.

Lunch is next.

Bathroom trip and washing up first.

Thank goodness! I am very hungry!

After you are done and cleaned up,
you may rest or read quietly
until everyone is finished.

When everyone is settled
and the music turns on,
it is time for nap.

After you have napped or rested,
you may play with quiet toys
until the lights turn on.

Time to wake up!
We clean up all of our things.

Let's go to the bathroom before we
start our next lessons.
I don't want anyone to miss them.

It is time to do some activities
and toy areas! I am so happy to
be making friends.

We will do different projects, crafts, science activities, and other fun things!

Now it is time for snack.
I will read you some stories
on what we are learning about.

Now we get to play outside again!
Our parents will be coming soon.

This is so much fun! I don't
know why I even worried!

Hey! My mom is here!

Miss Roy! My mom is here!

Hey Mom!!

Can I go back to school tomorrow??

I had a great, fun day!!

Let's talk about your day.

How did you feel when you started school?

Were you nervous or scared about anything?

What was your favorite part of the day?

Who did you play with?

What are you excited to do tomorrow?

What would you say to someone nervous?

It's okay to have feelings. Spread your wings and fly into learning new things!

More Stories from Rising Butterfly Press

Children grow, learn, and spread their wings through stories.

Discover more books written by Amy McDonough:

My Best Friend
A heartfelt story celebrating friendship, kindness, and the
joy of being yourself.

My First Day of Preschool
A comforting adventure that helps little learners feel brave and
excited as they begin their preschool journey.

My Family Farm Field Trip
A special trip to a family farm where children discover where food
comes from and why farmers are the real MVPs of the community.

More adventures coming soon!

Did you find the butterflies hiding in this book?